Anthems
for SA & Men

Contents

MUSIC DEPARTMENT

OXFORD
UNIVERSITY PRESS

OXFORD
UNIVERSITY PRESS

Great Clarendon Street, Oxford OX2 6DP,
United Kingdom

Oxford University Press is a department of the University of Oxford.
It furthers the University's objective of excellence in research, scholarship,
and education by publishing worldwide. Oxford is a registered trade mark of
Oxford University Press in the UK and in certain other countries

ISBN 978–0–19–351820–9

Music originated on Sibelius
Printed in Great Britain on acid-free paper by
Halstan & Co. Ltd, Amersham, Bucks.

Index of Orchestrations

The following accompanied items are available in versions with orchestra. Full scores and instrumental parts are available on rental from the Oxford University Press Hire Library or appointed agent, and also on sale, where indicated.

A Clare Benediction
2fl, ob, 2cl, bsn, 2hn, hp, str

All things bright and beautiful
2fl, 2ob, 2cl, bsn, 2hn, hp, str
Full score on sale (ISBN 978–0–19–341311–5)
Set of parts on sale (ISBN 978–0 19–341312–2)

For the beauty of the earth
2fl, ob, 2cl, bsn, 2hn, glock, hp, str
Full score on sale (ISBN 978–0–19–340727–5)
Set of parts on sale (ISBN 978–0–19–340729–9)

Look at the world
2fl, ob, 2cl, bsn, 2hn, hp, str

The gift of each day
Small orchestra version: 2fl, ob, 2cl, bsn, 2hn, hp, str
Chamber version: hp, org

The Lord bless you and keep you
Accompaniment for strings
Full score on sale (ISBN 978–0–19–340730–5)
Set of parts on sale (ISBN 978–0–19–340731–2)

for Clare College, Cambridge

A Clare Benediction

Words and music by
JOHN RUTTER

Also available separately (ISBN 978-0-19-341658-1), with an accompaniment for piano.

SOPRANOS and ALTOS

you; may his spi - rit be ev-er by your side._____ When you

A

sleep, may his an - gels watch o - ver you;_____ when you

wake, may he fill you with his grace:_____

May you

Commissioned by the Chancel Choir, First United Methodist Church, Omaha, USA, for Mel Olson

A Gaelic Blessing

Words by William Sharp (1855–1905)

JOHN RUTTER

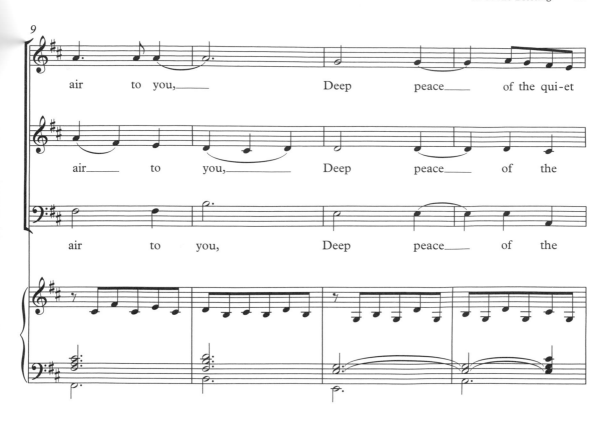

light_____ of the world to you,____

light_____ of the world to you,____

light of the world____ to you,

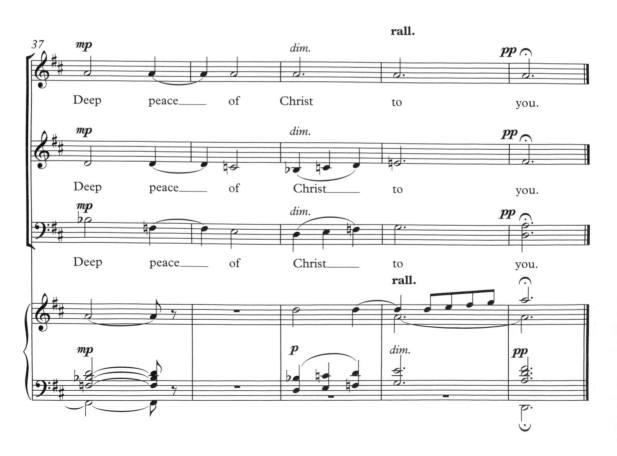

Deep peace____ of Christ to you.

Deep peace____ of Christ____ to you.

Deep peace____ of Christ____ to you.

God be in my head

Words from the Sarum Primer (1514)

JOHN RUTTER

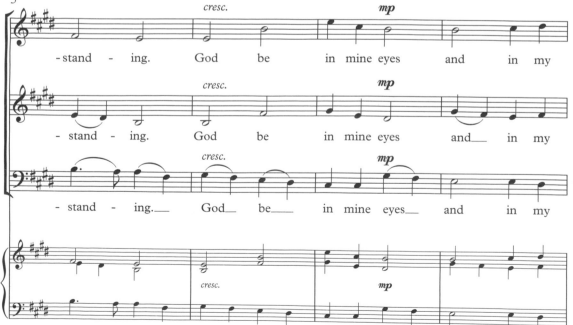

All things bright and beautiful

Words by Mrs C. F. Alexander (1823–95)

JOHN RUTTER

The Lord God made them all.
The Lord God made them all.
The Lord God made them all.

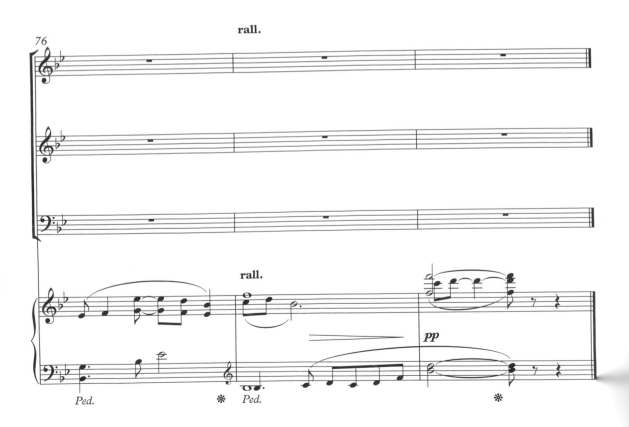

for Rosemary Heffley and the Texas Choral Directors' Association

For the beauty of the earth

Words by F. S. Pierpoint (1835–1917)

JOHN RUTTER

This our joy - ful hymn____ of praise.____

This____ our hymn of praise.____

This____ our hymn of praise.

B **MEN**

3. For the joy of hu - man

3. For the joy____ of__ love,

love,____

Bro - ther, sis - ter, pa - rent,

in celebration of the 70th anniversary of the Council for the Protection of Rural England

Look at the world

Words and music by
JOHN RUTTER

accompaniment is more suitable for piano, but it can be played on the organ.

Look at the world: so ma-ny   joys   and won-ders,

So ma-ny   mi - ra - cles   a - long   our   way.

A

SOPRANOS

mf

Praise   to   thee,   O   Lord,   for   all   cre - a - tion,

ALTOS

mf

Praise   to   thee,   O   Lord,   for   all___   cre - a - tion,

MEN

mf

Praise,   praise to   thee,   O   Lord,   for   all   cre - a - tion,

A

mf

(Ped.)

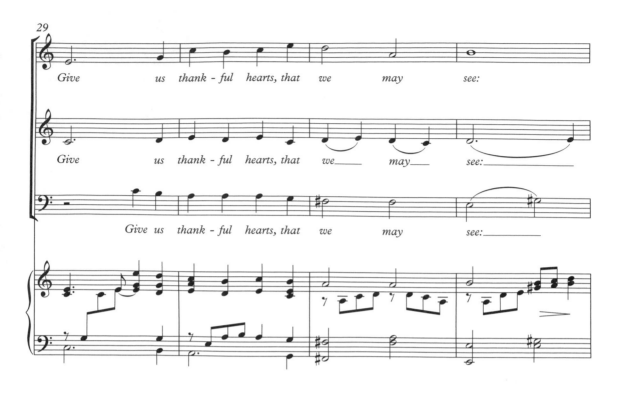

Give us thank - ful hearts, that we may see:

Give us thank - ful hearts, that we___ may___ see:_____

Give us thank - ful hearts, that we may see:_____

All the gifts we share, and ev - 'ry bless - ing,

All the gifts we share, and ev - 'ry bless - ing,___

All the gifts we share, and ev - 'ry bless - ing,

Lyrics:
All things___ come of thee.
All things___ come of thee.
All things___ come of thee.

B *unis.* **mf** SOPRANOS and ALTOS
2. Look at the earth

bring-ing forth fruit and flow - er; Look at the sky,___ the

(Ped.)

*Small notes are for rehearsal only.

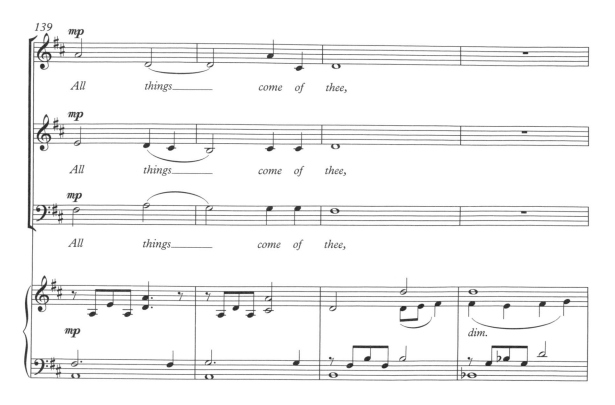

Commissioned by the Texas Choral Directors Association

Open thou mine eyes

Words by
Lancelot Andrewes (1555–1626)

JOHN RUTTER

*If low voices are available, men divide in these two bars.

37 -sire:___ Or-der my steps___ and I___ shall walk   In the

40 ways___ of thy com - mand - ments.___

The gift of each day

Words and music by
JOHN RUTTER

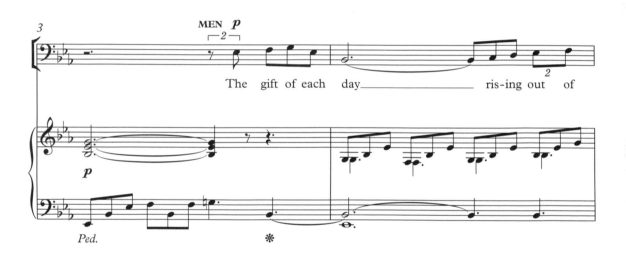

The gift of each day_____ ris-ing out of

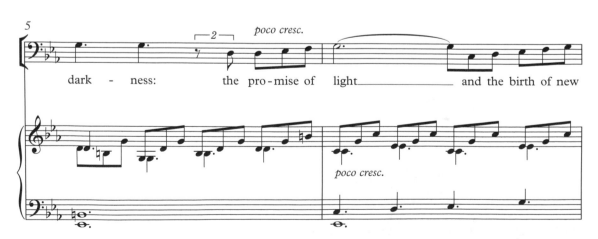

dark - ness: the pro-mise of light_____ and the birth of new

This anthem is the fifth movement of John Rutter's six-movement choral work *The Gift of Life* (ISBN 978-0-19-341150-0).

in memoriam Edward T. Chapman

The Lord bless you and keep you

Numbers 6: 24

JOHN RUTTER

Also available separately (ISBN 978-0-19-341659-8), with an accompaniment for piano.